Trading Strategies

Laura Bliss

Contents

INTRODUCTION

Options have become very popular, especially in the U.S. and they are far from being limited only to banks and specialist money managers, options trading for "retail" traders from all walks of life is now quite common. However, the idea of options is still being viewed with trepidation in some areas.

When I first started out on serious trading, a friend cautioned me of what I was diving into, but trading can be as secure as you want it to be. The truth is, you need a trading strategy that works. It helps to keep the risk low and your reward opportunity high.

You need the consistency and functionality of your strategy so that you can execute it with complete clarity every time. In the past few years, my trading plan has become increasingly easier and I would like to show you how you too can become successful with options trading.

CHAPTER ONE

WHAT ARE OPTIONS?

Options are often referred to as contracts. They give the party the right to purchase or sell a specific asset such as stock, real estate and merchandise for a specific price within a certain period of time. They also oblige a separate party to sell or purchase the specific asset.

An option is described as "the right, not the duty, to purchase (or sell) an asset at a fixed price before a predetermined date." In simple terms, an option is an arrangement that the buyer has the right to trade (the right to purchase or sell) the underlying asset at a predetermined price at a certain date.

What this means is that you know about the price of the stock you want to buy, regardless of the uncertainties that exist throughout the course of the contract. Commonly, one option contract is equal to 100 stocks of the company.

The unique part of the Options Contract is that it binds the buyer and seller to a deal of specific assets and conditions to reduce the risk of failure.

Options are also seen as financial securities that get their value from another underlying asset or financial measures. I will focus on stocks and stock market indexes. Options come in two ways, and they are call and position.

However, adding them to the existing investment and trading platforms helps you to take advantage of both bullish and bearish moves in any of the underlying options you pick. This would be the best thing to do since it would help you reduce your risk and it would also help protect your position. To better appreciate stock and index options, you will need to have a clear understanding of the asset in which they are built on.

This could mean looking at stock or index fluctuations differently. For example, Volatility is a core component of the option valuation. By comparing options to

the underlying security or other securities, the learning curve is built towards applying them.

The key reason for trading options is that you can leverage a large amount of stock for a smaller amount of money, especially with call options. Call options are often cheaper than the underlying asset, than put options.

Options are usually more competitive than their underlying instruments; this means that investors are having *extra value for their buck* or more activity. Clearly, this can lead to risk, but as you would see, it can also lead to more protection and security.

You will also find that this would enable a lot of stability in your trading and also give you the opportunity to make a profit even when you do not know the direction in which the stock is going to shift. In the case of a market downturn, investors with portfolios should set up security

Mechanisms

Look at the market

Tips

----

1. **Selling Covered Calls** - if you possess a stock, you can viably decrease the expense of that stock by selling secured approaches that stock each month. This is a strategy that stock traders ought not to be managing without, yet don't utilize it if you claim to stock for sentimental reasons - stock trading must be your business.

A long these lines, if you infrequently get got out and end up selling your inventory, you can rapidly proceed onward to the following one.

1. **Long Call**: This is the most common technique that is mostly used by casual buyers as a dive board for trading options. A long

call entails an investor purchasing a call option on an underlying asset that he or she

expects will rise considerably above the strike price before the expiry date of the option contract. If trade signals are correctly used (more on this in the next chapter), this technique will prove tremendously valuable, since it has minimal risk and unlimited benefit potential.

This call is relatively simple, has unlimited potential for profit and only limited risk. However If the value of the underlying security does drop, the buyer will lose the premium paid to secure the option and the option will expire as worthless.

1. **Short Call**: This strategy takes advantage of a bearish market and uses puts to gain monetary reward. While this strategy looks to be simple and good practice for options beginners, it is incredibly risky and for that reason is not recommended until the investor feels extremely confident in his or her ability to predict future market trends. However, the short call strategy will be included here to explain why it is a poor choice for new investors and how it can be used to an experienced investors

advantage. A short call strategy involves the investor writing a put option when he or she believes the value of a specific underlying security is about to take a dramatic downturn. In order for the investor to reap a profit, the value of the security must drop by more than the amount of the strike price to gain a profit. In order to gain a substantial amount of capital, the price would have to continue to drop and the buyer would still need to purchase the put by the expiration date; otherwise the seller is left only with the premium paid by the buyer to purchase the option. However, if the market has high volatility and the investor has not taken this into account, the value of the security may rally. If this occurs, then the investor will lose the premium gained for the sale and potentially limitless funds afterwards.

This is an easy strategy to apply and requires no initial investment on behalf of the seller. It can be extremely helpful if the investor is sure the value of the security will go down and confident the market will not

experience extreme volatility in the near future. However, unlimited losses could incur as a result of using this strategy. Even if the market does move downward, gain is limited. Again, this strategy is not recommended for new investors until they are practiced at predicting market trends.

1. **Bull Call Spread**: Investors use the words bullish and bearish frequently to characterize the emerging market conditions. When anyone refers to a strategy as being "bullish" in nature, they say that the trader carrying out the strategy assumes that share prices are or are going to rise. Which often refers to market forecasts, where a simple visible uptrend is alluded to as a "bullish market." Thus, the investor holds an option on the underlying asset, assuming that the valuation of the asset is going to increase, by way of a bull call spread. If the trader's calculations are right, they would be in-the-money, reaping a profit that is far higher than the strike price. Inversely, that is true of those who

have a positive mindset towards trading options. Sellers have a duty to purchase stock after all, traders cannot deal without goods and therefore expect the stock price to increase so that they can deal it at a higher strike price, thereby once again making a profit. It's also regarded as possessing a positive mentality. Traders should bear in mind that bull call spreads are mostly used for short-term calls. Below is an example of a bull's call array, also known as a vertical array. There is limited potential loss; traders cannot lose more than their initial investment. However, there is also a chance of limited potential gain. If the value of the stock skyrockets, the bullish trader will be forced to sell the stock for the strike price. They will still make a profit, just not nearly as much as they could have if they had not written the option.

1. **Bear Put Spread**: In contrast to the bull, if someone says they are approaching an option with a bearish strategy, it means they want or anticipate the price of the underlying asset to fall. If the trader is a buyer,

they want the price to fall because they have the right to sell the stock and they will be able to sell for a low strike price. The situation becomes much more precarious for sellers, who want the price to fall because they have an obligation to sell the stock. The main difference between the bull call spread and bear put is that after the trader buys a stock, he will write a second one for the same underlying asset with a strike price below what he bought. That is where the profit lies. There is also very little risk factor, with the investor only able to lose the initial amount invested in the spread. However the disadvantages is that as with the bull call spread, there is also limited reward potential. The investor cannot earn a profit higher than the value of the option he or she bought at expiration less the value of the option the investor sold and less again the initial investment.

1. **Covered Call**: Covered calls are a bullish strategy and a risky game to play that poses many pros and cons. Normally, a trader writes options

against stock that he or she already owns. While this results in a potentially hearty collection of premiums this is the amount paid by a buyer for the option, the seller runs the risk of being obligated to sell their stock. However, if a trader already holds a long position on a piece of stock that he or she feels bullish towards, it may be a good idea to give covered calls a cautious try. Covered calls should only be taken on though if the volatility of the stock is minimal. Simply owning the stock may not do much to increase profit, so participating in a covered call will allow traders to collect premiums, which can act as buffers in case of a negative move in the market.

1. **Long Strangle**: A long strangle strategy involves the investor purchasing both a call and put with the same expiration date and underlying asset, but different strike prices. Similar to the long straddle, the investor will feel confident that the market is about to make a fairly drastic move, but is unsure of the direction. In order to gain a profit, the

investor will generally need to place the strike price above the stock market price so that they are out-of-the-money. This strategy is another favorite due to its limited risk and unlimited potential for profit. Since the options are bought out-of-the-money, long strangle strategies are cheaper to implement. The life duration of the option allows for more time for the stock market to make a substantial move, and the larger the move, the greater the reward for the investor. Lastly, there is a relatively small amount of risk involved, as the potential loss is limited to the debt incurred making the trade.

1. **Butterfly Spread**: This strategy is a little more complicated than those previously discussed as it involves a combination of bullish and bearish approaches as well as four separate call or put purchases. To complete this strategy, an investor would need to purchase one out-of- the-money call/put, write two at-the-money calls/puts, and purchase one in-the-money call/put. Investors who use this strategy tend to anticipate

that the stock price will be relatively the same when the option expires as when it began, making this a neutral strategy. While this approach does tout limited risk, in which the investor can only lose as much as they put into the strategy, it does not have unlimited profit. Additionally, a complicated strategy such as this is usually completed successfully by more practiced traders. Trading via the butterfly spread allows investors to partake in only limited risk. Whatever the premium is that the investor pays to purchase the stock, which can also be partially offset by the sale of the two options at-the-money, is the total amount that the investor can lose
.

1. **Iron Butterfly:** This strategy is the much more complicated big brother of the butterfly spread; the iron butterfly involves using a combination of calls and puts. In addition to this, the investor must buy or sell a strangle while also combining the newly ac-

quired strangle with an existing long or short straddle approach. Simply, the investor needs

to purchase an out-of-the-money call, write an at-the-money put, write an at-the-money call, and buy an in-the-money call. Similar to the butterfly spread, the maximum profit is reached when the value of the underlying asset is equal to the strike price of the puts and calls agreed upon at the beginning of the various options contracts. Out-of-the- money options can be selected to cut down on costs and risks simultaneously. Because of the number of options and strategies involved, investors have the flexibility to change their investment plan halfway through the spread while still taking part in a limited risk strategy. This strategy is especially helpful for turning small amounts of funds into a rolling income.

1. **Iron Condor:** Like many other strategies, there are two subcate- gories of the iron condor: long and short. However, things get far more complicated than that. Successful application of the

iron condor involves holding both a long and short position in two separate strangle

strategies. This is achieved via a complicated web of puts and calls. To complete the strategy, investors will need to buy or sell calls and puts with the same expiration date that are all out-of-themoney in this order from lowest to highest: sell a put, buy a put, sell a call, buy a call. This particular type of strategy is most useful for practiced investors who believe the market will remain somewhat neutral. The length of time for which they believe this will hold true can be supported with either the long or short iron condor strategy. For the purpose of this example, the long iron condor will be featured. Profit is possible when using the iron condor. Any rewards reaped will be less than or equal to the net credit that the investor received upon beginning the trade, which means that it is possible for an investor to treat the iron condor as an insurance policy and continually be able to pay for it with calls.

These are all incredibly helpful strategies that a knowledgeable and intuitive trader can and will use to his or her advantage. However, there is one strategy not listed here that may be the most important of all, and that is an investor's exit strategy. It's a hard and fast rule to never enter into a contract without having an exit strategy, as the lack of one can cause some traders to panic when things begin to go south and lose a substantial amount of money. On the other hand, some rookie traders do have exit strategies and then get carried away with their success and abandon them, leading to later losses because they were, essentially, playing against the house. Investors who are serious about making a career out of options trading should always start with an exit strategy and adjust it to fit each individual situation. This will help to protect the trader against loss and increase portfolio revenue.

CHAPTER FOUR HOW TO SELL AND MANAGE YOUR PROFITS

Stock options trading has been available for about 40 years. Traders also gained an understanding of trading options and have provided

methodologies for trading options.

This may sound like a jumble, but try and use your imagination. There can be no strategies without a capacity to trade in a particular defense. These are the processes that offer rewards and, of course, misfortunes.

This occurs very much when a trader is in a typically odd place of benefit; however, he neglects to do so out of loss of mind or expectation that he would be higher or on some other basis. This plan is going to prevent this from happening. This strategy is also essential for the trading of online options. A

profit is a gain irrespective of where it is made. In the world of options, curiosity will emerge in just a few minutes, so it is best to ensure that it does.

Bear in mind, and you're handling your options. At a time when the economy is betraying your position, the majority of your earnings, in addition to a few or the entirety of your money, will disappear rapidly. You ought to act quickly, not to be afraid to pull the trigger. You are never going to be a penniless asset. You ought to take advantage of the options trading procedures. That's why you're going to execute them in any event. Concentrate on the plan, watch the market, and move on. This should make a return on the long term.

STEPS TO TAKE:

Look at the market

It is common knowledge that traders are causing their options to expire. This is true of traders who have been holding long positions. In order to make the alternative viable, the demand must hit a price. If a trader chooses to choose an

alternative, he/she may consider the likelihood that the demand will hit a certain amount. The cheap premium would not guarantee a decent deal of trade. A good market and opportunity means that this will be a good deal of investment.

You can watch the market for a certain period of time when you're looking to buy a stock option. See the trend and see if there's a chance to make a buck with that. If it is, then it's time to get there. If not, it might be best to sit that one out and not take the risk with it. You can watch the market by watching the stocks every day and seeing which ones are doing well, and which ones are going to stay away. **Think Monthly Distribution**

A lot of traders prefer to look at the premium option rather than the possible returns. Although it is significant, they tend to focus too much on it, and by so doing neglect the likelihood that the demand can meet and eventually exceed the strike price.

In most situations, it's best to keep trading options easy. In order to decide whether or not the option is a good trade, the trader can calculate the average monthly range of the market. It is a figure that provides a view on the uncertainty and the probability of hitting a break-even point.

The average monthly range can also be compared to other comparable inventories. You might see a stock that has a good trade opportunity, but the average range is bad, and there's no hope of benefit. But let's assume you see that one is a little higher than the other, but you find that there's a lot of potential for that stock. It's safer to go with the latter, because it can mean a potential increase in your own earnings, and it'll end up benefiting you more as a result later. **Use the average monthly set**

In order to calculate the average monthly set, the trader requires historical values. If the stock is used as the underlying asset, historic high , low, open and

close values can be restored within a certain period of time. The average monthly range requires the high and low daily values of a given stock. The average price can easily be calculated during the cycle when the demand fluctuates between the high and the low of a month.

In most cases, traditional traders are using open and close monthly values. The low price is subtracted from the high price during the month in order to obtain a number, which is then rounded up and divided by months.

OPTIONS PRICING MODEL

Here are a few pricing models to consider when trying to figure out the price of the product. All you need to do is fully consider a few good models, and then use an online calculator. This chapter is going to cover some of the basic models out there, along with how you can understand them.

The Concept of Black-Scholes

In 1973, Robert Merton, Myron Paddy, and Fischer Black developed the Black- Scholes pricing model as a form of luxury computing options.

Since then, this model has become the most common one. In reality, Merton and Paddy received the Nobel Prize in Economics two years after the death of Black in 1995. Black, though, was still remembered for his work, although he was not awarded the Nobel Prize because he was awarded the Nobel Prize to living persons only.

The Black-Scholes model applies only to the European options, both bid and put, and does not include paid dividends in its estimation. It can still be used, though, by using the ex-dividend value of the asset.

The model assumes that this option can only be used when it expires. And that's why only the European alternatives are being discussed. Furthermore, apart from not accepting paid dividends, this model also does not take into account any commissions.

It also assumes that the market is competitive and that market movements are volatile. Volatility and risk-free interest rates are stable and wellknown. Lastly, the Black-Scholes model assumes that returns are normally distributed. This alternative only takes into account one risky asset, such as a bond, and then a risk-free asset, such as cash.

With this, there is no possibility of settlement, but with this arrangement, there is a way for someone to borrow money at a risk-free rate. You can also purchase

any stock of this sort, even a fraction of it, without any hidden fees or prices. With this method, the derivatives are calculated at the current time, as well as the payout. You may create a long stock investment with a short investment option.

In order to calculate the option value, the Black-Scholes model requires the following: -risk-free interest rate conditional uncertainty, pacing (expressed as a percentage of the year), strike price, and the current price of the underlying asset. It's a complex mathematical formula. The average person may be frightened by using it. Luckily, online calculators are available and can be used to calculate the price using this chart.

In addition, there are statistical tools provided by trading platforms that are used to calculate the price. This is a good way to estimate the purchase, but it is not the only thing you should be relying on. Due to market volatility, liquidity threats and sudden changes and hazards, you may be vulnerable to some major risks. There are also extreme price shifts, and most of the time, money doesn't come with an unchangeable worth in the real world. It's a good way to get a sense of what you're about to do, but at the same time, you're not expected to rely entirely on that.

Cox-Rubinstein Binomial Price Option Approach

Mark Edward has created a variant of the Black-Scholes model, the Cox-

Ross- Rubenstein model. It's Rubenstein, Stephen Ross, and Carrington Cox. The key advantage of this model is that it uses a lattice-based model that takes into account the price movements of the underlying asset over time.

The lattice-based model takes into account shifts in the different variables over the life of the option. It results, thus, in a more accurate price choice. It looks similar to a flower, which advances to the depletion of the stock in this way.

This model is used for American options. It implies that everyone is oblivious to risk, so that returns are equal to the risk-free interest rate. The Cox-Ross- Rubenstein model also assumes that arbitration is not feasible because the system is completely efficient.

The price of the underlying asset can never rise and fall simultaneously. It can only be achieved in one direction at any given time. During the life of the option, different points in time can be defined. Because of this, a binomial tree can be formed.

Normally, it is measured from the beginning of the option to the end of the option, and then back again. Once this is done, it will be calculated on the basis of the parameters of the increases in dividend rates, along with the changes in option prices.

All of this is measured together and put into a theoretical model to help others understand where their money is going. The biggest advantage of

this is that it

applies with American stocks. Another advantage is that it also lets you see precisely where the stock is at a particular point. You should take a look at this, and through the predictive properties of it, you'll know where the stock is going to be in the future. In that respect, it's beneficial.

The biggest limitation, however, is that it takes time to calculate. You are looking at a bunch of numbers all at the same time, and many older computers can't do it.

However, as technology changes, software is able to keep up with the speed of changing numbers. It's recommended that you get an online calculator to see where the stock will be at a certain point in time.

Like the Cox-Ross-Rubenstein model, online pricing calculators and analytics tools provided by trading platforms can be used to calculate the option price.

The Balance Put / Call pricing model

The put / call parity was introduced by Hans Stoll as a pricing principle in 1969. According to his report, there is a connection between a European call and options with a common strike price and the expiry date. This means that, for each call option value at a given strike price, there is an acceptable option value for that call option.

The same goes for the set values of the option. There is an acceptable call option value for a specified option value at a certain strike price. The relationship exists because a position is formed, which is the same position as the underlying asset when there is a mixture of set and call options.

The returns must be identical for the underlying asset and the option so that the arbitrage does not occur. Traders and investors who take advantage of arbitration will make a profit if the opportunity arises. Set / call parity is used

to assess pricing models for European options. If the outcome of the pricing model does not meet the parity check, this means that negotiation will take place and the formula must be dismissed as a pricing strategy. There are a number of ways to measure set / call parity.

Luckily, several trading platforms provide analytical tools. They have visualizations of comparisons between call and call. But of course, you don't have to memorize all the pricing models. Only choose one that suits the case, have a convenient online price model simulator, and let the numbers shift for you

CHAPTER FIVE WHY OPTION TRADING IS BETTER THAN STOCK TRADING

Options trading has been the focal point of much discussion of ongoing years. Is it risky? Would we be able to go bankrupt? For sure, options as a type of subsidiary instrument is unmistakably more perplexing than the stocks that they are composed dependent on and, similar to a wild stallion, can hurt you if you don't see how it functions and how to utilize it appropriately.

This conveys us to the point of this section. In this part, I will exhibit 5 reasons why options trading is, in reality, superior to anything stock trading to scatter the well-established legends of how perilous options trading is.

We should recollect this: Options trading is hazardous just when you don't get it. Below are the various reasons why options trading is more preferable.

1)

Variable Leverage

The influence that options gives you is maybe the principle motivation behind why individuals incline toward options trading in any case. Power is the capacity to accomplish more with a similar measure of money.

Trading options enables you to make a lot more benefit on the same proceed onward the hidden stock. When you buy the commodity itself without edge, you are merely making 1% benefit on a 1% move to support you.

In any case, in options trading, you could be making a 10% benefit on that equivalent 1% move the stock made or even up to 100% on that equivalent 1% move!

Indeed, the excellence of influence in options, not at all like in prospects trading, is that it is VARIABLE! You could take on more influence for more hazard or lesser importance for lesser danger by picking options of various strike costs and additionally termination month.

By and large, the more out of the money options, the higher the influence and the more in the money options, the lower the influence.

Influence cuts the two different ways. This is the reason the excellence of control in options trading is that it enables you to do similar trades with a lot lesser money, all things considered, you could primarily utilize just money you can bear to and plan to lose in any fizzled trade for every alternative, so influence really help you control your misfortunes!

2)

Bet Downwards Without Margin

To benefit from a downwards proceed onward a stock in stock trading, you could short the stock which causes edge. In options trading, all you have to do to wager on a stock going downwards is to BUY its put options with no margin required by any means.

It's hard to believe, but it's true, buying put options for the benefit to drawback works precisely equivalent to buying call options for the benefit to the upside.

There is no compelling reason to possess the stock previously, and there is no requirement for the edge! **3) Multi-Directional Profits**

Stock Trading

In stock trading, you possibly benefit when the stock goes toward the path you need it to. Upwards when you buy the stock or downwards when you short the stock. There is no real way to benefit in the two situations at the same time, and there is no practical way to help if the cost of the stock does not move.

Nonetheless, in options trading, such multi-directional profits are conceivable! Some options methodologies enable you to benefit regardless of if the stock goes upwards or downwards rapidly, and there are options procedures that profit irrespective of whether the cost of the capital stays unaltered!

Such is the pure enchantment of options methodologies which enormously builds your odds of winning in options trading versus stock trading!

Play Banker

Weary of continually being at the player's side of the table? In options trading, you could change slightly to the investor's side of the table and do what market producers do by selling options to individuals who are needs to take the bottom of the player!

At the point when the players lose, as they frequently do, you get the opportunity to keep the wager as a benefit only like a genuine investor! Just options trading has the "wager," which you had the opportunity to, and it is known as "outward esteem."

CHAPTER SIX THINGS YOU SHOULD KNOW ABOUT OPTIONS TRADING

When you start trading options, you'll feel like you're being bombarded with a lot of details. This is right. But if you want to get the momentum going from the start to stop those defeats for beginners, you need to have a few tricks up your sleeve to achieve an edge. And the benefits / leverages are the only thing that can get you the money you seek, at the end of the da y.

Although, most people will believe there are some sort of "secrets" that make rich people wealthy and don't let the other trading win. But that can't be too far from the facts. In truth, all the secrets you'll be reading here are common sense and all rely on your ability to understand and apply certain things.

Patience and self-discipline are the best secrets of all (yes, including life). You want to make sure that in every exchange you learn new things, and that the understanding of a specific topic is continually growing. You are going to be tested this way but in a challenging and constructive way.

Take your time because you're new to all of this. Think of it this way:

After only one lesson, can you feel yourself qualified to do brain surgery? Yeah, the same goes for stocks, and more so for selling options (though the same rules apply). Treat yourself to studying.

You are doing exactly that by reading this novel, giving yourself a learning opportunity. If you already know stocks, then this is the next step. And just when you first had to be familiar with trading securities, you now have to be familiar with trading futures, too.

In addition, if you're happy enough to sell, you'll need flexibility to do the exchange itself. We've also had the feeling of moving too early into an undertaking even when we weren't fully sure it was the best thing to do. Be careful, take a deep breath if you need to and still stick to your trading schedule. Last but not the least, persistence often includes choosing a trade plan where time works in your favour and where the drawback is protected. There are lots of techniques in this book for you to pick from so you can still try to keep it simple.

Which one you choose, still wait to get the right chance to introduce yourself. I hold to a few chart trends to sell and if they don't turn up, I don't have to sell. Specialist professionals make the most of the profits. So, specialize in what you're commercializing.

Be positive with your mindset towards accumulating money. The more careful you are therefore, the better it would be for you. That isn't about sitting back and doing nothing.

You need to persevere. If you believe in something, you must commit to it before you accomplish your objective. And then set another target after you have achieved your objective. Having embarked on the task of becoming a successful trader (whether full-time or part-time), to get there, you have to stick to that. Anybody can do it. I have seen that with my students' time and time again, where the most unexpected characters can become phenomenal traders

— even those who don't believe they can.

Offer yourself manageable expectations in a reasonable time period, to be rational. But by next week you will be thoroughly acquainted with the risk profiles of the four major choices. It's likely you will do it tonight. Keep setting goals that are attainable (but find them a minor challenge), so you can keep up the excitement of learning and gaining knowledge.

You are just going to start increasing your confidence as you go along, reminding yourself of your ability to grasp everything you're worried about.

The greatest insight is from learning. It's all too well to say, *"Mechanically, deal,"* but very few people do it.

Emotions are part of our nature, but instead of denying them, it is more productive to work with them. That's what my trading plan is all about remaining secure, but still being able to play for big wins.

Know that learning is dependent on experience. We can always remember the most serious of our school teachers, right? You can recall the funniest, the scariest, the most fragrant, the prettiest, and the ugliest, but I'll bet you are having trouble recalling something about the teachers who were in the middle those that hardly had an experiential impression on you after years of being in the same classroom. The same happens to commerce.

Most of the research involved with investing is focused on experience. In reality, the most important method of learning about trading is experience-based. It's through traumatic situations where you find out more about yourself

in good times and difficult times. Many of the great merchants had awful encounters, but most importantly, they went up to the challenge and applied what they knew. Just like me, man. I made a lot of money really soon, I felt I was invincible, and then I gave some of it back easily. Trust me, I didn't feel too good after it, so I knew.

More specifically, I used the tutorials. So, let yourself get your insight, which is what this book and my seminars are all about. At the end of the day, I 'm sure you'll end up going back to the logic found in my trading strategy.

Honestly you have to be frank with yourself if you wish to become a good trader or investor. In the end, the scores decide how successful you are. Your decisions are your responsibility, not anyone else's. Blaming other people will never support you. If you pull the trigger, you 're the one in charge.

Hedging is one of the most important parts of the exchange in options. Remember, for example, that you are buying an alternative position and that

you are still retaining your present position. After the buy, if you believe the stock is going to rise, you can easily purchase 10 call options to make a profit.

But what if the world is playing a game against you, and the supply isn't going higher? You'll end up spending the money as the options come to an end. But with hedging, you can turn the loss into advantage by buying 5 options while things are going against you. Yeah, even if things go extremely wrong for you, you will still make a good out of it.

There is another hedging tactic called a covered call. You own the underlying stock in this strategy, and you sell a bid to that stock. When you're selling the offer, you accept that you're going to fund the value of the stock at the trigger price of the contract.

This means that the burden on your investments is transformed to an advantage, which ensures that you spend less money as things hit the fan.

One thing you should know about every exchange is that you should use everything in your

arsenal and have as much leverage as you can to make a profit. Making the best of the various strategies and choices you have. Plus, exploit the protection you get by selling options.

Traders and buyers who pursue a particular plan, regardless the business environment, are typically the ones who get terrified of the stock market. They keep saving and don't sell until there's a big shift in the fundamentals. This is absolutely wrong if you want to make a fast buck and escape long-term risks.

Also, there's never a "all-purpose" approach that some traders use. In this situation, you need to go with the trend and adapt to market conditions. In addition, let the market conditions lead you in the right way.

More likely than not, you are going to make a buck. This means that you can never miss the chance to acquire calls, spreads, and mails. But of course, before you buy all of it, you should know what's going on in the economy. This is

where the analysis is coming into play. Always have an exit strategy. This should go without saying something.

You're still expected to be ahead of the curve and have an escape plan in place. It doesn't matter whether you're winning or losing. A good exit strategy will help you reduce your losses when things go south.

Plus, it also lets you get rid of some of the trades that keep sucking in your earnings. On the other hand, the escape plan still stops you from losing money in the future. This law is fundamental for any form of investment. You want to make sure you walk out of the situation with a grin and a decent amount of money.

Study until doubling down. It's enticing to double your earnings when you know the trading is going according to your schedule. Until again, terrible things are going to happen. And that's why you want to make sure you are ahead of the curve.

You work out the patterns, and so you capitalize on them to keep yourself from losing. Make sure you know the pattern is stable and you can expect it to get your money. Even after that, you are supposed to have an exit plan all in place to save yourself should things go south. Don't ever play catch-up when it comes to trading options because you're going to end up losing your portfolio.

It might be quick to open a new trading account for options, but it's not worth the task. You should try to stay low and learn ropes before you launch, and then steadily increase the risks you take. And with time, you are going to be able to enjoy a trading lifestyle.

Don't wait too long to buy back your short options. It doesn't matter if you're just hoping that you'll be able to squeeze the tiny benefit out of the trade, or if you're just waiting for the contract to expire worthless.

You're never expected to wait too long to buy back your short choices.

Buying short options early is much easier than dwelling on why you made the same

mistake again. If you think that a trade is going to get out of hand, and you should buy back your short option to the risk and bring an end to a benefit selling, so do so immediately. It's going to be worth the extra amount you are spending.

CHAPTER SEVEN THREE KEYS TO SUCESSFUL OPTIONS TRADING

In the new dynamic and actively negotiated market for futures, losses are made on a regular basis. Learners are losing money a lot more easily than they used to in stock markets, and the slightly impeccable options approach appears to be too similar and so far away.

All in all, the main investigative questions that traders are now presenting are, what exactly does it take to be successful in trading stocks?

Here are five keys to the Options Trading Accomplishment that I have achieved over a period of selling options.

1.

Understand the demands of your business

One of the great things about buying stocks is that there is not just a standard form of investing. If you can manage your emotions and have enough resources to exchange in the middle of the day, you could decide whether to exchange or push trading options on a day.

If you are like the vast majority of people who would like to buy and sell it a few days or weeks after the event at a cheaper discount, you might be able to swap trading options.

If you are technically disposed of and you may like to put yourself in a situation of fixed unsurprising profits, you might have to learn more and more about role trading.

Day trading, force trading, swing trading and position trading are four main ways to trade options. Choosing which solution to follow is basically part of the measure of time you will take and of your preferences. **2. Understand the approach you have selected**

There are also various ways to benefit from day-to-day investing, swing trading or position trading strategies. These methods have gone from simple to simple. Irrespective of what technique you are aiming for, you must thoroughly understand the procedure; the benefits and drawbacks as well as the hazard profile.

This combines the most important advantage and disadvantage, as do the circumstances under which they exist. Understanding the options approach goes beyond just acing the counts but, still, seeing how you can react to all the possible outcomes of the scheme.

Continuously trade in paper for an extended time, with the intention that you learn each of its advantages and drawbacks before applying for real money.

3.

Choose the Best Stock

Any preference technique profits when the underlying stock succeeds with a specific target in mind and losses value when the stock fails to do so. Irrespective of the approach that you want to follow, you should generally choose stocks that work in the same way.

In this range, key principal and advanced review skills are important to the achievement of trading options. The technical inquiry is of vital interest in the trading of options, as the exact passage and leaves are essential to options, being a time-consuming financial instrument.

CHAPTER EIGHT

TRADING SIGNALS

Trading on the stock market may be daunting. With so many potential contracts out there, it's hard for traders to know which ones they should buy or sell, and which ones they should let go of. In times of increased trade and market uncertainty, traders are dependent on trade signals to help determine their next steps.

Trade signals derive mainly from technical indicators, which are "any collection of metrics whose value is derived from the common price activity of a commodity or asset.

Technical indicators are most commonly used by active traders on the market, since they are primarily intended for the study of short-term price fluctuations" (Investopedia, Technical Indicator).

In addition, charts which shape bearish or bullish pennants which further allow traders to determine the value of options and forecast market movements. Various signals will be deciphered in this chapter, and examples will be given to illustrate how investors can use signals to their advantage.

If all this sounds a bit like a hockey fortune-teller reading tarot cards, don't worry; as with all the material on the market, it's actually pretty scientific. A last recommendation is to look at old main patterns over a long period of time and get an understanding of where the trading signals are coming up and how the market responds and them. With practice, investors will be able to identify the map signals quickly.

Flags

This first example of the trading signal is relatively easy to understand. The flag symbol is rectangular in shape, very small, and normally slants in the opposite direction of the market trend. It's a brief moment when the market breathes and remains relatively calm before the pattern of the previous flag begins. This moment of stability before the trend continues is called the period of consolidation.

Once the flag has been spotted on a bullish pattern of continuity, investors will decide to start buying calls, as the share price is low and investors expect it to rise in line with the trend. Find a flag on a trend line by scanning where two parallel lines precisely match the visible market trend.

It's Pennant

This map is a short-term trend of continuity of the line. With a pennant pattern, the symmetrical triangle refers to an increase or decrease in the trading trend, depending on whether the pattern is bullish or bearish, respectively.

In general, a pennant is shaped just after a flag symbol, and is sometimes referred to as a flag pennant. Since the aim of a trading signal is to determine when it's time to buy or sell, using a bullish or bearish pennant pattern to forecast market trends can further warn which tactics to use to retain or improve properties.

Rectangle

Rectangle exchange signals are very similar to flags with one exception: unlike flags, the rectangle signal has a much longer and more stable convergence duration.

In general, this means that investors may have a reluctant stance towards the market during the consolidation period. The trend would calculate the attitude of the participants (a.k.a. desire to sell and buy), resulting in a normal horizontal pattern that is closely compacted between strong market trends.

Looking at the trend line, buyers would easily be able to see where the long rectangular boxes are in the line and use it to make market forecasts.

W edge's

Wedges fall into the following two categories: rising and falling. They may then appear in a bullish or bearish pattern. The tricky part of the wedge is that for a beginner, the market price will continue to rise at first sight.

However, once the trend line splits out of the wedge, it moves in the opposite direction as it was in the wedge. This means that investors, generally speaking, realize when they see a fork that the market is starting to move in the other direction.

This is the moment when many buyers will continue to launch new strategies to take advantage of the change in the market.

Head-and-Shouder

This signal is used to determine when the pattern will become saturated and reverse itself. It shows a clear equilibrium within the market as sellers bring down the trend line and buyers push it back up again.

This signal can be representative of an upward or downward direction, depending on the current business conditions. The stock will usually rebound three times; the pattern will change its bullish or bearish stance after the last shoulder (or third peak). Like other signs, investors can use this knowledge to buy or sell calls and make calls when appropriate.

Any early investors who are frightened by trade indicators choose to become representatives of online signal suppliers that investors can pay in order to be alerted to any potentially major shifts in the market that investors can then use to their benefit.

Unfortunately, as the saying goes, nothing in this world is free. Trade signal providers will cost a considerable amount of money, as the best trade signal providers take risk management into account and provide customers a range of services that will work out the needs of each individual in terms of trade priorities, funding and start-up capital.

However, consumers should always be careful of signing up for services offered by signal providers. The Internet is riddled with scams and, more often than not, a seemingly trustworthy signal provider seems to be incorrect only a few months after being advertised as one of the best signal providers available.

A clear warning sign that a customer is joining the scam is that the provider offers facilities free of charge. In comparison, deceptive places may ask the trader to spend a certain amount of capital that the trader is likely to lose.

Even if the investor believes that he or she has discovered a secure site, in-depth research must be carried out prior to the purchasing of membership at any signal

provider site. The threats are too high to knowingly enter into a contract and are similar to trading options before reading a book about it.

CHAPTER NINE RISK MANAGEMENT AND HOW TO RECOVER YOUR

LOSSES

Risk management is very relevant for traders in options. It's what any trader in options should realize, because if you don't, it can cause issues later on. This chapter will analyze some of the better risk control techniques for successful traders to help avoid snags later when it comes to trading options.

Plus, once you get these down, you can use them to secure your capital, and they're going to save you a lot of issues now and later. ***These are the things you need to do to manage your risks***

Economic Preparation

For all in your life, the first thing you need to do is prepare. From fighting, to what you're going to do afterwards, planning and preparation is how you get to the top. It's the preparation that will get you there, and good traders schedule their trades before any sort of trading starts. Planning accordingly is the distinction between defeat and defeat.

Stop-loss and take-profit are two ways to help you prepare ahead of selling options. The seller decides the price that they are prepared to pay to sell options, to they calculate the return against the likelihood that the supply will meet the predicted amount. When they have enough of it, they

're going to sell it.

Unsuccessful traders don't really glance at what they're doing, or have a strategy because they're selling in order to make a profit. They don't know if the options market is going to change, and as a result, they're like competitors with the options they have.

They may have an unfair streak, and then passions may take over. Emotions are not part of the trading of futures, they are just preparation and policy. If losses arise, people hang on and decide if they want their money back, but still they continue to make the same mistakes. If you think before you deal, you'll end up at the top of the exchange.

Stop-Loss & Take-Profit Clarified

You've seen what those two words are, so you should know what they mean. It's important to have a good understanding of this, because as a merchant, it can be the deciding factor of making a deal and making a profit and not being able to do so.

Stop-loss is the price at which the seller sells a stock and suffers a trading loss. This is anytime the trade doesn't work like they have hoped. This can hopefully discourage the "going back" mindset and minimize damages when it gets to work. For example, if the stock breaks before the stage, the trader will sell it as soon as possible in order to avoid losing anything.

A take profit is the same price that the seller would exchange the stock in order to make a profit. It's when the alternative hits the price they want. That is when, considering the threats, the payoff is reduced. If the stock moves upwards at a resistance stage, the trader's options may sell it before the meeting takes place.

Calculation of returns

Another way to help set up a stop and take points is to help you measure the estimated return. It's necessary, because you can think of the trend instead of the trend. Rationalizing this. It would also provide you with a structured way of comparing trading and selling at the most profitable moment.

This will give you a chance to see what the anticipated return will be. It can help decide whether to sell, along with the chances of gain or loss, along with helping to make an informed guess.

This risk control techniques can help keep problems from getting worse. It's important to know this, because it's something any investor can take stock before they start investing stock options. This reduces the chance and lets you get to the top.

Taking part in trading stocks, there are some risk management strategies that will help you plan more and make life easier for you. This chapter will cover nine unique items to look out for when trading options, and why each of these nine options is relevant for trading options. You should be able to do this to ensure accuracy in the selling of options, along with tremendous performance.

Allocation flow downstream

The first definition is the division of money. You're expected to make sure you're not pouring anything into one thing. You should make sure that you don't place your entire investment portfolio in equities, but not in shares, real estate, and commodities. You should also strive to ensure that the diversification even extends to groups.

Some start assuming that they're just going to bring their stocks into equities like Apple or Google. However, if you don't position it somewhere, it will make your portfolio overweight in one region. You should also make sure that this does not interfere with each other, even though you own both stocks and mutual funds. You should look at the business and what it carries before you invest in it, because you may end up spending too much in one place.

The explanation that you should take care of this and make sure that you correctly distribute it is that the more stable the portfolio ensures that there will

be fewer gains or losses in the event of uncertainty. In recent years, though, the downturns might be associated, so make sure that if they occur,

You're saving, don't place it all in one market. If you put anything in real estate, it might end up losing you, just is the case with several buyers after the 2008 housing bubble collapse.

Seeing Global Risk Capital

You need to take care of the total risk money. If you are buying options, you should be vigilant to raise the total risk capital by more than 15-20 per cent. This is because if you let things go, you're putting yourself at risk, because you may have too much on the table. You'll still need to brace if a stop-loss happens to you, you may lose more of your money than you planned. That's why you ought to make sure that your portfolio just has so many, even if it goes beyond behaving accordingly.

Watch Account Option

If you have an opportunity portfolio, you need to watch how many you have on the market. You should make sure that at any moment no more than 50 per cent is on the market. It's dangerous to even get 50 percent on the market, so maybe it's better to get less than you can.

Catching the singularities

For a single strategy, you can make sure that it does not reflect more than 5% of portfolio options.

In the danger side of it. If that place continues to struggle, it won't hurt you if it's that number. That's how it will typically fall down to only 2.5 per cent, which is about a 50 per cent drop. It's easier to make sure you're not bringing too much into one field than depending on one way to save it all.

Manage the currency

Managing capital is crucial to this. You've just got a small number to use, so you've got to maintain hold of it in order to prevent it from being lost forever.

The easiest thing to do is position-size, which is when you decide how much you want to invest in certain options.

By doing this, you can decide how much you want to spend, and how much of an amount you're going to bring into something. You can only use a small sum so that you don't depend on a single result.

Few trades can turn out to be bad, but if you do things right and just put a certain amount in it, you'll be able to determine how much you're going to bring in and how bad the future losses will be.

Managing Orders

If you choose to handle the risk in an easy but efficient way, you will use a range of options to position your order. In addition to the four major order categories, you can position various orders of options to assist with risk control.

You can look at what's going to help you, because occasionally it will help keep you from selling at a better price. There are instructions that you can immediately lock in benefit to reduce losses.

For example, if you have a limit stop command, it can be regulated as you leave the place. This would help you eliminate situations where you lose out on gains from keeping a role too long, or prevent any significant losses because you didn't blackout quickly enough.

HOW TO RECOVER YOUR LOSSES

Recovery is a vital process to ensure that your personality is right and that you learn from your mistakes. But first of all, you want to make sure that you've gained enough information to help you learn from other errors.

In this part, we are going to focus on how to rebound from your defeats and why it's important to have a clear mind and keep things simple, particularly when they're rough.

You ask yourself, "How do I restore my account and reduce the percentage of damages I have suffered? When you start losing trades, you start thinking there's a quick step you should take to get rid of all that and get back to winning trades and getting the money you like.

But that's a deadly mistake. You should never make sudden changes to the way you deal because, in the long run, you are going to lose a lot of money.

You should understand that the business has no plot against you. There is no guarantee that you can restore your account immediately.

This is how you are slowly and steadily restoring your trading account so that you have learned everything along the way and become a better , stronger investor.

1. Stop trading on real money It might sound insane and unproductive, but you've got to stop it right now. This will keep you from wasting any more money because of the mistakes that you've made in the past. Give yourself a break to calm down and accept that you've lost a lot of trades. One of the reasons I'm telling you to stop trading is that you might be dealing in vengeance, which is the best way to lose all the money you've got.

2. Open up your head Now that you've stopped trading, use this time to clear your mind and decide what's going to cost your money. When you find out these things, you can notice that you really feel good, because now you know that you can close the distance. For some people, the loss would be a psychological thing. If you're one of those, then you want to make sure you get back in the right way of thinking before you get back to trading. You want to be confident and optimistic when it comes to

trading. So stop being over-confident and pessimistic, because that's what ends up in defeats.

1. Now that you've learned stuff that result in losses, you can try different strategies and ideas in your trial account to make sure they 're working in real life. Use this time to really nail it down to know exactly what action to take in different situations to make a profit and win almost every trade. It's like a day of rehearsal. So make sure you survive these hours and remember that you're

doing it because this will keep you from losing thousands of dollars in real-life trades. Demo trading will also help you get in the correct way of thinking because when you start winning trades in your test accounts, you'll improve your confidence when you're trading online. Once you see that you're doing incredibly well in your demo account and you've corrected your errors, it's time to get back to real trading.

HOW KNOWING GREEK MIGHT JUST

HELP YOU UNDERSTAND OPTIONS

BETTER

The Greek option offers you the advantage of the anticipated changes to the contract, including the changes in the underlying stock. They are derived from one of many option valuation models and are available from a number of websites, such as the option calculator.

Many Web Sites Share Options are supported with this application. You enter the price of the underlying stock, the option strike date, the time to expire and the option quote using the option calculator. The calculator then sets out each of the Greek values given.

The perspective that you learn from the Greeks is as follows:

Delta: reflects the anticipated shift in the option value of any $1 rise in the price of the underlying stock. Gamma: This reflects the estimated change in Delta for any $1 change in the price of the underlying stock.

Theta: Reflects the predicted regular decrease of the alternative due to time. Vega: Reflects the potential shift in option value due to changes in the price expectations of the underlying stock.

Rho: Calculates the adjustment in option value due to changes in the risk free interest rate (usually T-bills). Optional market adjustments due to interest rates are far lower, which ensures that the above factor gets fewer attention.

Option pricing models can be used to assess whether a given alternative is comparatively costly or inexpensive. The model is better applicable when you accept its implications and acknowledge that Greeks have desired qualities that do not in any way guarantee the future.

Delta is perhaps the most important Greek value for you to grasp initially because it explicitly links changes in the underlying stock value to increases in the option value. Delta values are as follows: Calls: 0 and

1.00 or 0 and 100 Calls: 0 and – 1.00 or 0 and – 100

Gamma will provide you with the estimated change in delta for any $1 rise in the price of the underlying stock. By knowing and testing gamma, there's less risk that delta values will get away from you.

CONCLUSION

Thank you for reading this book to the end. The next step is for you to apply everything you have learnt. I hope this book would be able to help you become the success that you are.

www.ingramcontent.com/pod-product-compliance
Lightning Source LLC
Chambersburg PA
CBHW071518210326

41597CB00018B/2806